ELEMENTARY SCHOOL LIBRARY
OCTAVIA - UNIT 8

"Poppies in a Vase" by Hong

cover painting, "Carnival Parade" by Carolyn Jablonsky

ELEMENTARY SCHOOL LIBRARY
OCTAVIA - UNIT 8

I Paint the Joy of a Flower

by BILL MARTIN JR. with paintings by Carolyn Jablonsky •
Helen Winslow • Hong • C. P. Montague • Stanley Maltzman
• R. W. Davidson • Buffalo Kaplinski • Audrey Menicucci •
Ronald Thomason • Irving Shapiro • Jackson M. Hensley •
Howard Bobbs • Arthur Hall • A. W. Dowl • Frank Riley •
Seong Moy

ESPECIALLY FOR MY FRIEND, GENE D. SHEPHERD

front end sheet painting, "Palos Verdes" by Helen Winslow

back end sheet pastel drawing, "Lily Pond" by Seong Moy

Copyright © 1970 by Bill Martin, Jr. • Published simultaneously in Canada • Printed in the United States of America • Library of Congress Catalog Number: 74-111206 • All rights reserved. Permission must be secured for broadcasting, tape recording, mechanically duplicating or reproducing in any way any part of this book for any purpose. • SBN 03-084576-9

HOLT, RINEHART AND WINSTON, INC. New York, Toronto, London, Sydney

"Texas Blue Bonnets" by C. P. Montague

*I paint
the joy of a flower,*

"Maple Road" by Stanley Maltzman

the flaming of leaves,

"Mountain Scape" by R. W. Davidson

the boldness of mountains,

"Wild Poppies" by Hong

*the dance
of a breeze,*

the aloneness of prairies,

"Adobe Corrals and Fences" by Buffalo Kaplinski

"Seascape near Carmel" by Audrey Menicucci

the break
of the sea,

"The Empty Swing" by Ronald Thomason

the silence of summer,

the age of a tree,

"Winter's Peace" by Irving Shapiro

"Rockport Landscape" by Stanley Maltzman

the circling of seagulls,

"Winter Arrives" by Jackson M. Hensley

the dusting of snow,

"Monterey Regatta" by Howard Bobbs

the lure of the water,

"Winter in Santa Fe" by Arthur Hall

the
blue
of
shadow,

"Mountain Autumn" by A. W. Dowl

the brilliance of aspens,

the shyness of streams,

"Western Sunset" by Frank Riley

*the glory
    of sunsets,*

*the wonder
    of dreams.*